Magic...Naturally!

Also by Vicki Cobb

SCIENCE EXPERIMENTS YOU CAN EAT

HOW THE DOCTOR KNOWS YOU'RE FINE

ARTS AND CRAFTS YOU CAN EAT

SUPERSUITS

Magic...Naturally!
Science Entertainments
& Amusements

by Vicki Cobb
Illustrated by Lance R. Miyamoto

J. B. LIPPINCOTT COMPANY

PHILADELPHIA AND NEW YORK

U.S. Library of Congress Cataloging in Publication Data

Cobb, Vicki.
  Magic . . . naturally!

  Includes index.
  SUMMARY: Scientific principles are explained and demonstrated by
using them to create magic tricks.
    1. Science—Experiments—Juvenile literature.   2. Conjuring—
Juvenile literature.   [1. Science—Experiments.   2. Magic tricks]
I. Miyamoto, Lance R.   II. Title.
Q164.C49   793.8   76–13179
ISBN–0–397–31631–3   ISBN–0–397–31632–1 (pbk.)

TO MARSHALL KARP—

WHO KNOWS THE DIFFERENCE BETWEEN ILLUSION AND REALITY

AND THAT MAGIC IS BOTH.

Contents

1. Be Phenomenal! 13

2. Mechanical Wizardry 21

3. Fluid Fascinations 47

4. Energy Enchantments   83

5. Chemical Conjuring   109

6. Perceptual Puzzlements   135

Magic...Naturally!

1

Be Phenomenal!

You can take nature into your own hands and be a magician! You can amaze and mystify your friends by doing the impossible. You can amuse them by showing them curious oddities. The key is to use the laws of nature so you appear to defy natural laws. It's not hard to do. Nature is full of events that can be dramatic and entertaining, even magical, when you present them in a special way.

Magic is all in the way you view a phenomenon. Imagine putting a solid white object into a transparent liquid and watching it disappear before your eyes. Amazing! Or is it? Actually, you do it every time you put a lump of sugar in a cup of tea. A commonplace event, unless you take a closer look to see what happens when sugar dissolves.

Both sugar and water are made up of very small particles called molecules. The molecules in sugar and water are constantly *moving*. The molecules in a lump of sugar are vibrating in place and water molecules are tumbling over one another. When sugar and water come in contact, water molecules move between sugar molecules, separating them from one another. This is what happens when something dissolves.

In everyday life, dissolving a lump of sugar is hardly entertainment. But suppose you use the lump of sugar to hold a spring in a coiled position. Then you put the spring in a teacup (without letting anyone see what you're doing) and rest a spoon on it. Then, when you pour on hot water and let nature do its thing, you create magic. The sugar dissolves, releasing the spring. All your audience sees is that you pour hot water into the cup and the spoon jumps out. Experience tells us this is not possible. Your performance of the impossible makes you a magician.

Science & Show Business

People learn what things do by observing everyday events. If you let go of an object, it falls. Strike a match and it burns with a yellow flame. Grape juice remains purple when you pour it from pitcher to glass. Magicians make ordinary things act in unexpected ways. When a magician lets go of an object, it might fly up instead of down. A match might burn with a snakelike ash or flash brilliantly like a firecracker. Grape juice might turn green when poured into a glass. The unexpected is an important part of good entertainment.

Scientists often find their work surprising and entertaining. They get their kicks by figuring out what's happening to make objects fall, or have a certain color, or burn. They use many methods and approaches to solve nature's mysteries. And when they find out what's making an event happen, it's sometimes not what was expected at the beginning of the search. Who would have thought something no one can see, taste, smell, or touch is largely responsible for a flame? The discovery of this stuff, oxygen, and of its role in fire came as a surprise. Thin strips of iron are not a fuel. Yet, if they are heated and put into pure oxygen, they burn as wood burns in air.

Science and magic are not strangers to each other. Long ago there was popular interest in odd natural events such as the power of a rock called a lodestone to attract iron from a distance, the power of a glass disk to make near objects seem far away, and the power of certain herbs to cure illness. The study of these phenomena was called *natural magic*. It was believed that hidden forces were the power that made these events happen.

Science, as we know it today, became separate from natural magic as some people developed methods for discovering the real causes of natural events. Natural magic came to be used as entertainment and was performed for audiences by people called conjurers.

As science grew, new discoveries were often presented to the public. A poster for a hit show, taken on tour from Europe to colonial America in 1753, read in part:

FOR THE ENTERTAINMENT OF THE CURIOUS
Featuring a wonderful bottle that can . . .
1. Draw a piece of money out of a person's mouth in spite of his teeth, without touching him or offering him the least violence.
2. Melt metal (though without heat) in less than a thousandth of a minute.
3. Kill animals instantly.
4. Make a bright flash of real lightning dart from a cloud in a painted thunderstorm.

The star of the show was *electrical fire*, better known today as *static electricity*. The bottle that produced it had been developed eight years earlier. It was known as a Leyden jar and was used to collect enough static electricity to produce a giant spark—the same kind of spark you get when you brush your hair on a cold day or take synthetic fabrics out of a dryer; only this spark was much bigger. The Leyden jar was one of the first tools used by scientists to understand electricity. And, for a while, until people became familiar with the wonders of artificial "lightning," it was, as they say in show business, "box office."

As a laboratory tool, the Leyden jar proved to be a curtain raiser to the understanding of electricity. Benjamin Franklin developed the theory that there is an "electric fluid" in objects. He used this theory to explain how the Leyden jar works. Later he demonstrated that the spark produced by a Leyden jar (static electricity) is the same phenomenon as lightning.

What's Happening Here

This book contains instructions for performing some amusing, puzzling, and exciting magic tricks. All of them are based on natural events. Some were known to conjurers hundreds of years ago. Others come from phenomena discovered by scientists in the course of their investigations. The idea is to learn something about science by performing for the entertainment and amusement of your friends.

Each chapter deals with some of the phenomena of a particular science. Beginning with physics, you can learn something about mechanics, the behavior of liquids and gases, energy, chemistry, and perception, which is part of psychology. You'll learn more if you read the book in the order it is written. Often the principles used in one trick are a part of the principles in a later trick. In each case there is a brief scientific explanation of what is known of the phenomena that make a trick work.

Learning to perform magic tricks from a book is like learning to play tennis or a musical instrument by reading a book. You can have fun following the directions here for your own amusement. But turning your performance into entertainment is another story.

There are no rules to tell you just how to be entertaining. The best advice is to practice a trick until you feel comfortable with it. (You might want to try it a few times in front of a mirror.) Choose the time and place for the performance of a trick carefully. Some effects are amusing if they happen in a casual and spontaneous way. Some are suitable for an informal magic show for your friends.

The things you say during your performance are an important part of your act. Make up a story around a trick or work it into a good joke. Since you are probably not a professional actor, you will be more effective if you act like yourself. Bring your own personality to your performance rather than pretend to be like stage magicians with top hats and tails. If you act naturally while performing natural wonders, you will find people are entertained. To help you we've suggested some performance tips for each effect in the book.

One last thing. Remember, once you know how to do a trick the mystery is gone for you. You may be surprised to see how easy it is to make others wonder. Keeping an audience guessing is one of the chief in-gredients of magic, and professional magicians have sworn not to tell their audiences what makes their tricks work. However, you might want to make an exception to this rule when performing the tricks in this book. One of the exciting things about these tricks is understanding the science behind them. You can make your performance even more entertaining by asking your friends if they can figure out why a trick works and then letting them in on the explanation after you've kept them guessing for a while.

This book can get you started on an adventure. It's an opening to science, entertainment, and magic—a natural combination. It's what's happening here.

2
Mechanical Wizardry

Suppose you saw someone throw a ball into the air and it never returned to earth. Would you believe your eyes? Or would you think there was a trick someplace? Magicians and scientists both know that our senses can be fooled.

Take the case of a rolling ball. A ball rolling along the ground rolls more and more slowly until it finally comes to a stop. We've all seen this happen. Yet a man named Galileo, who lived in Italy in the seventeenth century, looked at the behavior of a rolling ball and thought, "This doesn't make sense."

He reasoned this way: A ball that rolls down a hill picks up speed, going faster and faster. A ball rolling uphill rolls more and more slowly until it stops for an instant before rolling back down the hill. A ball rolling on level ground should not speed up (because it's not rolling downhill) and it should not slow down (because it's not rolling uphill). He concluded that a ball rolling on level ground should keep rolling forever. It should *not* stop. The fact that a rolling ball *does* come to a stop made Galileo wonder what was happening. He was one of the first to take a second look at moving objects and question what he saw.

Physics is the science that grew from the kind of questions Galileo asked. The part of physics that deals with the motion of inanimate bodies is called *mechanics*. The natural laws of mechanics describe how objects move and how forces upon them affect them. More than once they show that we can't always believe what we see. You can fool your friends with the tricks in this chapter.

Pulling the Impossible: Inertia & Friction

You challenge a friend to remove a strip of paper that is between a stack of poker chips and the cap on a soda bottle. The chips must not be touched or caused to topple. Result: crash after crash. Then you, a true believer in natural law, pull off the job.

Galileo looked at a rolling ball and asked, "Why does it stop rolling?" He also looked at a ball at rest and asked, "Why doesn't it move?" Years later an Englishman named Isaac Newton came up with an answer to both questions. His theory is called Newton's First Law of Motion. Simply put it states: Moving objects will remain in their state of motion and resting objects will remain at rest *unless an outside force acts upon them.*

The outside force that makes a ball rolling on a level surface stop rolling is friction. Friction is the force that makes two surfaces in contact with each other resist moving past each other. Friction between the bottom chip of the stack of poker chips and the paper it rests on is strong enough to cause the chips to move when the strip moves.

Now suppose you could eliminate the friction between the paper as it moves and the bottom chip. What do you think would happen to the resting state of the stack? The answer is: nothing. The force needed to move the paper can only move the chips through friction, as there is no force acting directly on the stack of chips. If you can get rid of the friction, the chips will remain in place.

It's easy to think away friction. But in the real world you can't get rid of friction completely. You can reduce the friction between two surfaces, for instance by using a lubricant, such as oil, or by making both surfaces very smooth. In this trick you reduce friction by moving the paper very quickly. The less time two surfaces are in contact, the less friction there is.

> a strip of paper about 1½ inches wide and 3 inches long
> a soda or catsup bottle with a cap
> stackable objects such as poker chips, checkers, or coins

Place the strip of paper on top of the bottle so that one end is longer than the other. Stack objects on top of the paper, making a big show of how easy it is to knock them over. A high pile is heavier and harder to start moving than a stack of only a few objects. As long as there is some stability to the stack, a higher stack works better and makes the trick look more difficult. Challenge someone in your audience to remove the strip without knocking over the objects. After each attempt fails, set the stack up again.

To remove the strip quickly, moisten your index finger (so it briefly sticks to the paper, providing better contact), grasp the longer end of the paper between your index finger and thumb, and bring your hand down fast.

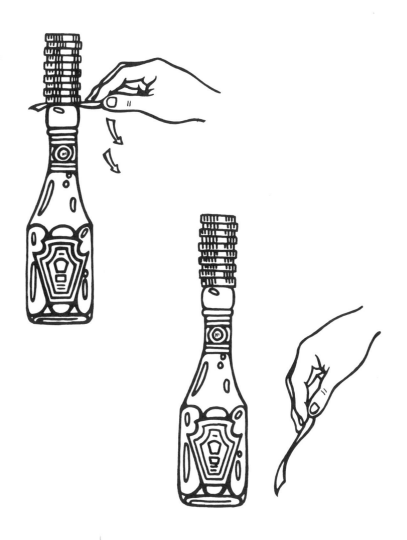

Performance tips: This is a good trick to perform for a friend in an informal manner. You can also use it effectively in a tabletop show for a small audience.

Fill a glass two-thirds full of water and cover it with a playing card. Balance an egg, with the larger end down, upright in a ring of aluminum foil on the card.

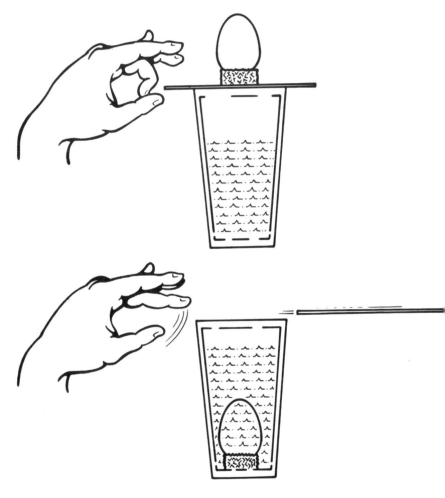

Place your middle finger against your thumb, then flick the card out from under the egg. The sharp blow makes the card fly off. The egg falls into the water unbroken. Break the egg later to prove it was not hard-boiled.

Make a ring of stiff paper by gluing the ends together. Place it on top of a soda bottle. Balance the cap on top of the paper ring so it lines up with the top of the bottle. With a flick of a pencil (or a magic wand if you wish) whisk the ring away. The cap will drop neatly on top of the open bottle.

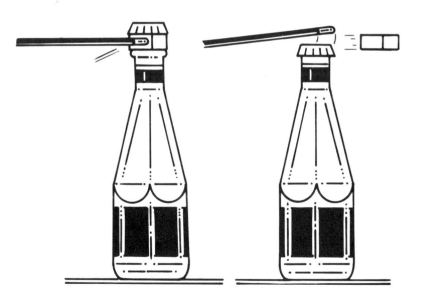

On a smooth surface, stack ten black checkers and one red checker, placing the red checker second from the bottom. Stand another red checker on its edge and shoot it at the stack by pressing on the top and then letting your finger slide down along the edge. The checker should scoot out from under your finger. With practice, you can make a direct hit so that the curved surface of the moving checker delivers a blow to the red checker in the pile. The red checker is knocked from the pile without disturbing the black checkers.

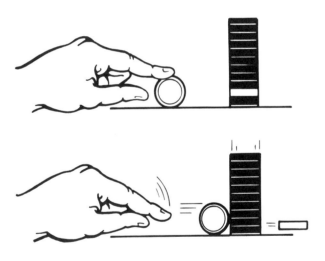

Karate Payoff:
What Force Is About

A swift karate chop with a dollar bill breaks a pencil in two. Your friends soon learn that money has that kind of power only for you.

WHAT'S HAPPENING

When one object strikes another, each object experiences a force equal to the *mass* of the object delivering the force times the change in speed (*acceleration*) of the object delivering the force.

It's easy to see that an object with a large mass can deliver a larger force than an object with a smaller mass. A sledge hammer can break rocks more easily than the household variety hammer. But small objects can also deliver a large force if they are moving fast enough. A bullet, for example, can shatter a brick. A sports car traveling at eighty miles an hour can do more damage in a collision than a truck traveling at five miles an hour.

A karate chop is based on this principle. The hand (which doesn't have great mass) delivers the blow so swiftly that the force on impact is great enough to break a brick or a block of wood. If the struck object breaks, the hand is not injured since it doesn't receive the force of the blow. If the struck object doesn't break, however, the hand receives the force of the blow, and the result is painful.

THE SETUP & THE ACT

> a long wooden pencil
> a dollar bill
> a willing friend

Announce you can break a pencil with a dollar bill. In an open manner, fold the bill lengthwise. Ask a friend to hold a pencil securely at each end. Make sure your friend's grip is firm.

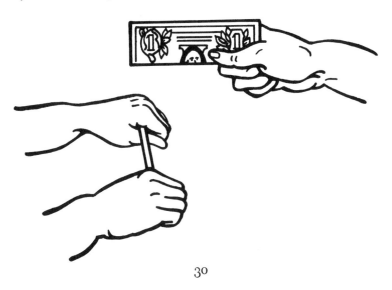

Hold the folded bill at one end between your thumb and the first joint of your index finger. Your hand should be a loosely curled fist.

To dramatize the feat, raise and lower the bill over the pencil twice while counting, "One . . . two . . ." As you bring your hand down on the count of three, straighten your index finger so you can deliver a karate chop to the pencil. Be sure to move your hand down as swiftly as possible and don't hesitate before impact.

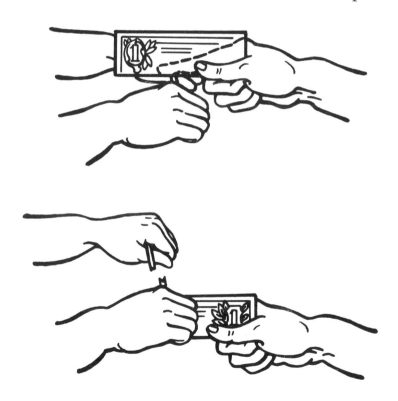

Be sure to curl your finger again after the blow has been delivered so your audience won't guess how you broke the pencil.

Invite others to try to duplicate your action with another pencil.

Performance tips: Practice karate chopping pencils without the bill until you become confident the pencils will break. Then practice with the bill so you can get the timing of extending and withdrawing your finger. This trick is good for spontaneous, casual fun with a friend as well as for an informal show.

Supertough Tissue Paper: A Non-Elastic Collision

Would you believe you can use all your strength to ram a tightly stretched piece of tissue paper with a broom stick and it *will not tear*? Your friends won't take your word for it. Read on.

WHAT'S HAPPENING

Motion can be transferred from one object to another during a collision. It's this fact of nature that makes a billiard game possible. When a cue ball collides in a direct hit with a resting ball, motion is transferred. After impact, the cue ball is at rest. The other ball moves away, reaching almost the speed the cue ball had before the collision. The slight loss in speed is partly due to friction and partly due to a very small amount of heat energy which is generated on impact. A collision between objects where no energy of motion (kinetic energy) is lost is called an *elastic collision*. As collisions go, in our imperfect world, an encounter between billiard balls is pretty elastic.

Needless to say, there are many collisions that are not very elastic. A moving body can exert a force on its target that can bend it out of shape instead of making it move. When a rigid object strikes a rubber surface (or when a rubber object strikes a rigid surface), the force bends the rubber out of shape temporarily. As the distortion returns to normal, the object bounces away. In other cases, such as when a wad of clay is thrown on the floor, the distortion on impact is permanent. All the force is used to change the shape of the object and there is no transfer of motion.

In this trick the tissue paper is protected by a material that can absorb the total force of a collision. The substance that does this is none other than table salt.

a paper tissue
a cardboard tube from a roll of paper towels
a rubber band
salt
the handle from a broom

Separate the two plies of a tissue in front of your audience. Be sure to display them so everyone sees how delicate they are. Stretch a single ply over one end of the cardboard tube and hold it in place with a rubber band. Pour in salt to a depth of at least three inches.

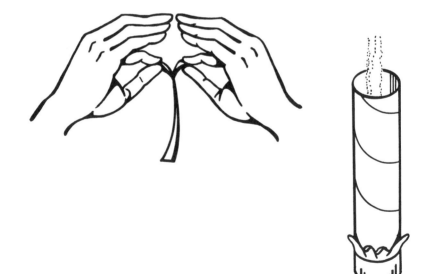

Announce that you will ram the broomstick down, the tube without breaking the tissue. Then do so with all your strength. (Hamming it up a bit here can add to the show.) Invite others to try. No one will be strong enough.

Here's how it works. There are a great many tiny air spaces between salt particles. On impact, the salt grains are packed closer together. This absorbs the force of the collision, so there's none left to tear the tissue.

Performance tips: Some tissues are stronger than others. Practice this trick before you try it in front of friends. You may find you'll have to use both plies if the tissue is very delicate. But try adding more salt before you decide to use an unseparated tissue. This trick is fun to experiment with if you're visiting with a friend.

The Haunted Hanky: Levitation with a Lever

An ordinary bandanna takes on a life of its own as it stands unsupported, defying gravity, then falls and rises again on your command.

WHAT'S HAPPENING

A lever is a rod that is free to turn on a point called a *fulcrum* and can be used to lift a weight with one end when a force is applied to the other end. A seesaw is a familiar example of a lever that has a fulcrum at its center. When no one is on a seesaw, it can be balanced with both ends the same distance from the ground. If a force is applied to one end only, that end moves toward the ground and the other end moves up. Both ends move the same distance, and the force with which the free end moves up is the same as the force applied to the end moving down.

Now suppose the fulcrum is much closer to one end of a lever than the other, as is the case with a crowbar. If you push the long end down a certain distance, the short end moves up a shorter distance. But the force the short end can apply is much larger than the force needed to push the long end down. For this reason, a crowbar is useful for doing jobs such as removing nails from wood.

A lever with a fulcrum closer to one end than the other can also be used to make the long end move up faster than the short end moves down. If you step on the short end of a crowbar, the long end flies up. The long end moves through a larger distance than the short end in the same period of time. So it moves faster. Baseball bats and fishing rods are levers that magnify a small motion on the short end to a longer and faster motion on the other end.

In this trick you use a hidden lever to make an object seem to rise on its own.

THE SETUP

> a bandanna about 22 inches on each side, made of material you can't see through

37

a needle
thread the same color as the bandanna
paper drinking straws

Turn up one side of the bandanna three-eighths of an inch. Stitch along the edge, leaving both ends open.

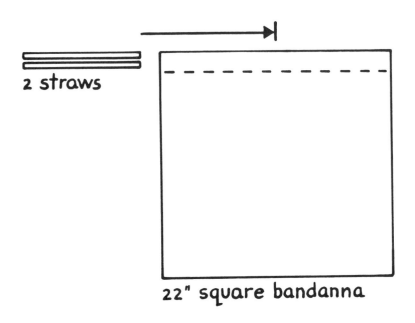

2 straws

22" square bandanna

This kind of hem is called a casing. The casing should be just wide enough to allow you to insert two flattened paper drinking straws. Insert the straws in one side of the casing, pushing them just far enough in so they can't be seen.

Have the bandanna tied around your neck. Make sure the straws are not in the part of the bandanna you tie. Arrange it so it falls in a natural way without bending the straws.

Untie the bandanna and hold it by the two corners of the casing with the straws on the right side. With-

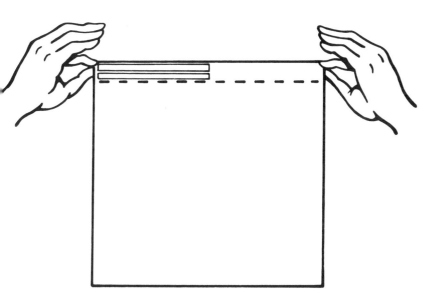

out moving your hands together, show your audience both sides of the handkerchief. Drop the right-hand corner and let the bandanna fall, still holding the other corner with your left hand. Tie a large knot in the bandanna near the left-hand corner.

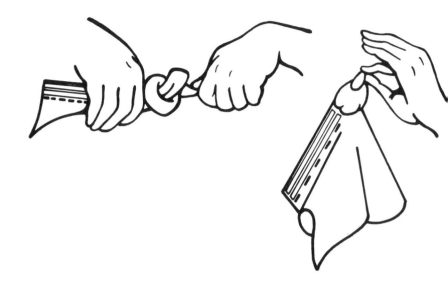

Hold the knotted part with your left hand and pull the handkerchief through your right hand with a gentle motion. Then hold the knotted part with your

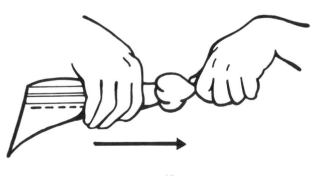

right hand and make the same stroking motion once or twice with your left hand. At the end of the final

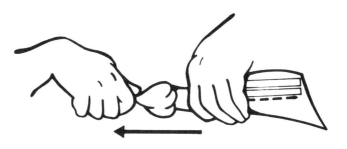

stroke, hold the bandanna with your left hand and let go with your right. The straws will hold it upright in the air.

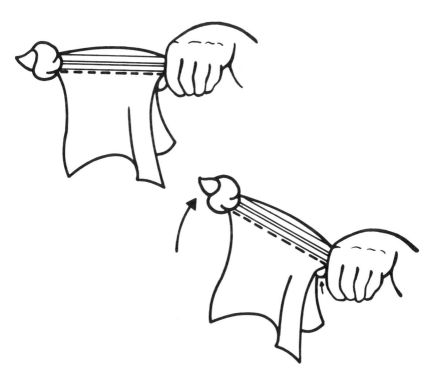

Now slide your left thumb over your left index finger in a small motion that moves the bottom of the straws. The straws are stiff enough to act as a lever and will slowly lower the handkerchief and raise it again. A little practice before you perform this for anyone will quickly show you the right moves. No one will notice the small motion you must make, because they will be watching the large motion made by the other end of your straw lever. If you wave your right hand in a magical way as you command the hanky to rise and fall, the illusion of levitation is complete.

When you have finished, untie the knot, roll the bandanna into a ball, and stuff it into a pocket.

Performance tips: If you want to impress your friends, wear your bandanna to school one day. Then, at the right moment, perhaps at lunch, claim you have magical powers. In an offhand way go into your act. They will be used to seeing the bandanna around your neck and will have no idea that you have spent time preparing for this moment.

The Strange Straw:
A Shift in the Center of Gravity

You pass out straws to your friends and ask them to balance the straws across their fingers. Your friends find they must put a finger under the center of a straw. Then you do a balancing act with your finger decidedly off-center. Curious, how strange it looks.

WHAT'S HAPPENING

There is only one place you can put the fulcrum (See *The Haunted Hanky*, pg. 36) so that a seesaw is balanced when no one is on it. The fulcrum must be right in the center of the board. That's because the board has a regular shape and its weight is evenly distributed throughout. The point at which you put the fulcrum so a lever is balanced is the lever's *center of gravity*. If you put the fulcrum at any point other than the center of gravity of a seesaw, the longer end will move toward the ground and the shorter end will move up. The seesaw is no longer balanced.

If you put a weight on only one end of a seesaw, you can balance it again in one of two ways: (1) By putting an equal weight on the other end. (2) By moving the fulcrum to the new center of gravity, which is a point off-center and closer to the end with the weight. Some seesaws have several notches near the center so the fulcrum can be moved to balance two people of unequal weights.

A paper straw, like a seesaw, has a regular shape and its weight is evenly distributed. Its center of gravity is also at its center. The straw you balance has had its center of gravity secretly moved with the help of a hidden weight.

THE SETUP

> a box of paper straws
> a tiny lead fishing weight

Put the fishing weight in the end of one of the straws. It should fit snugly so it won't come loose.

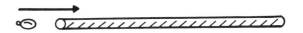

Put the straw back in the box, making a mental note of its exact position. Close the box and, if it came with a cellophane wrapper, see if you can replace the wrapper to make it look as if the box is brand-new.

Open the box of straws and pass a few out to your friends. Ask them to balance the straws across their index fingers. Then you remove the straw with the weight and place it over your finger. (You should practice a bit beforehand so you know where to place your finger.) The straw will be perfectly balanced, although your finger will be fairly close to the end with the weight. You can also rest the straw on a table with the unweighted end sticking way out over the edge.

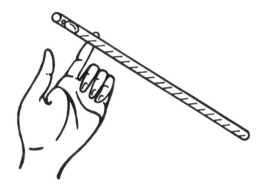

Performance tips: This trick is most effective when friends are over for a visit. You can spring it on them when you're having refreshments.

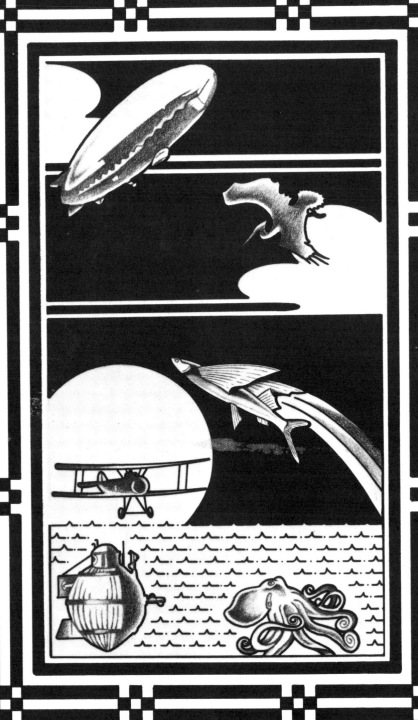

3
Fluid Fascinations

There's a natural wonder around that's totally invisible. Not only can't you see it, you can't smell it or taste it either. It creeps into every space that isn't already occupied by something else. And it's available to assist you in your magic act. As a magician, you can't do much better than to use the services of an invisible assistant.

Air is what we've been talking about, in case you haven't already guessed. Air is a gaseous form of *matter*, the stuff of our universe. Matter exists in three forms: solid, liquid, and gas. A solid has a definite size and shape. But liquids and gases, called *fluids* (from a Latin word meaning "to flow"), take on the shapes of their containers. A liquid has a definite volume; it takes on the shape of its container, except for its top surface. A gas does not have a definite volume. It takes on both the shape and volume of its container, spreading out to fill it completely.

Air and water are the fluids we are most familiar with. But they both have properties many people don't know about. Air seems like very flimsy stuff, yet it has weight which can be put to work. The surface of water acts like a skin that can be made to perform in some curious ways. The tricks in this chapter are based on the properties of some fluids, matter that has a way of seeming curiouser and curiouser the more you get to know about it.

Heavy Reading: The Weight of Air

The blow of a broomstick breaks a slat of wood sticking out from the edge of a table. No big deal. But wait . . . The wood is held in place with nothing more than two sheets of newspaper. Now news is not a weighty matter, or is it?

WHAT'S HAPPENING

The secret of this trick is that air has weight which presses on all surfaces. Although it seems as if air is very lightweight, if you get enough of it, it can exert a substantial force.

Air envelops the earth in a layer that is thickest at sea level and gets thinner and thinner as you move higher. Most of the earth's air is within the first five or six miles above the earth's surface. Above that it gets so thin its weight is very little.

The weight of a five- or six-mile column of air pressing on one square inch at sea level is almost 15 pounds. That's about the weight of twenty-two average-sized cans of soup. You can easily figure out the weight of air pressing on a sheet of newspaper 30 inches by 22 inches. Its area is 660 square inches. If about 15 pounds is pressing on each of these 660 square inches, the total weight on the newspaper is 660 times 15 pounds, or 9,900 pounds!

The newspaper doesn't tear, even with all that weight on it, because fluids press in all directions. The pressure of air on one side of the paper is the same as the pressure on the other side, so the paper isn't being pushed in either direction. But you can take advantage of the air pressure on one side of the newspaper by making sure there is as little air as possible on the other side.

THE SETUP & THE ACT

    an inexpensive foot-long ruler or a thin slat of wood

two sheets of large-sized newspaper
a broomstick

Place the slat of wood on a table with half of it sticking out over the edge. Show your audience how the wood flips off the table if you strike it without holding it down.

Place two opened sheets of newspaper over the part of the slat that is on the table. Smooth out the paper with your hands so as little air as possible remains between the paper and the tabletop. (The smoother the tabletop, the better the seal under the newspaper. This trick doesn't work as well on a tablecloth.)

Deliver a blow to the wood with the broomstick in a swift karate chop. The idea is to deliver the force so swiftly that the wood is broken before it has a chance

to act as a lever and lift the paper. If air gets under the paper, the weight of air on the top surface will not hold down the slat.

Performance tips: You might enjoy talking about the science behind this trick to a friend.

The Clinging Cup: Support by Air Pressure

You place your left hand on the bottom of a cup, mutter a few magic words while massaging the back of your hand, and—lo and behold—as you raise your hand the cup clings! The closest inspection cannot reveal a trace of sticky stuff.

WHAT'S HAPPENING

One way to get one object to stick to another is to use a suction cup. Air is forced out of the shallow bowl of a rubber suction cup when it's flattened against a surface. When the cup is released, it snaps back into place, leaving less air (which exerts less pressure) inside. Such a space, where some air has been removed, is called a *partial vacuum.* A suction cup sticks to a surface because the air pressure outside the bowl is greater than the air pressure of the partial vacuum inside. So the cup is held to the surface.

A suction cup sticks better if the edges of the cup have a good airtight seal. If there is leakage, outside air seeps in, quickly equalizing the pressure, and the cup loses its grip. Often a little moisture can be used to fill in any spaces of an irregular surface where air could leak in.

In this trick you make a suction between the bottom of a cup and your hand.

THE ACT

The only prop you need for this trick is a cup that has a shallow, circular, bowl-shaped hollow bottom. The size of the hollow bottom should be considerably smaller than the palm of your hand: two inches is about right. The cup should not be too heavy and the bottom should be fairly smooth.

To bring this trick off properly, you must make it seem as if you are going to do something very difficult that requires a great deal of concentration.

Announce that you have strange powers over the teacup. Place the cup upside down on a table and stand before it. Make a motion as if you were pushing up your sleeves as you get ready to perform. Then moisten the fingertips of your right hand with your tongue (the way you would moisten your finger to turn a page) and brush your hands together so your left palm becomes moist. Do this several times while you talk about how difficult it is to communicate with a cup. A moist palm is an absolute necessity if you are to have an airtight seal between your hand and the cup.

Place your moist left palm firmly on the bottom of the cup. Start rubbing the back of your left hand with the palm of your right. The idea here is to apply enough force to the palm of your left hand to push out the air. If you lean forward slightly as you rub (to add some of the weight of your body), no one will notice the pressure you are applying to the left hand.

If you have a proper seal, the cup will stick to your hand. You can raise your hand with the cup clinging to it, turn it over, and wave the cup in the air. The suction will not hold very long, though. Practice beforehand so you have an idea of how long the cup will stick. During your performance, release the cup with your right hand before the seal breaks.

After you release the cup, give it to your audience for their examination.

Performance tips: This trick is for a show with a small audience. Don't be afraid to ham it up. It's also fun to perform informally after dinner. It is, however, one trick that must be practiced till you get the feel of it.

Gathering Waters:
About Vacuum Cleaning

You challenge your friends to rescue a coin covered with a thin layer of water without wetting their fingers. The water may not be poured off the coin nor tilted away from it. Would you believe the tools for saving this money are a match, a birthday candle, and a glass?

WHAT'S HAPPENING

If you empty a pail of water onto the floor, the water quickly spreads, flowing into even the smallest cracks in the floor. Air also flows into spaces not already occupied by air. The sound you hear when you open a vacuum-packed jar of coffee or peanuts is made by air rushing in as the seal is broken. The motor of a vacuum cleaner creates a partial vacuum in the bag. As air rushes in to fill this space, it sweeps up solid material in its path.

In this trick you create a partial vacuum by burning a candle in a closed space. When a candle burns it uses oxygen, which makes up about 20 percent of the gases in air. (Most of the rest of air is another gas called nitrogen.) The flame goes out when all the oxygen has been used. The pressure of the air left in this closed space is less than the pressure outside. The water you want to remove from the coin is between this partial vacuum and the outside air. Like dirt being swept into a vacuum cleaner, the water can be pushed up into the closed space by the pressure of outside air.

THE SETUP & THE ACT

    a small piece of clay to act as a candleholder
    a birthday candle
    a coin
    a shallow dish (such as a glass pie plate)
    water
    red or blue food coloring
    matches
    an 8-ounce glass

You can set this trick up right in front of your audience. Make a candleholder out of clay and place the candle in it.

Place the coin in the dish and pour in enough water to completely cover the coin. Add a few drops of food coloring to make the water more visible. Challenge anyone to remove the coin without tilting the dish, pouring out the water, or using an instrument to touch the coin—and without getting wet fingers.

When your audience has run out of ideas, announce that you will accomplish this feat with the aid of a candle, a match, and a glass. Place the candle in its holder in the dish as far from the coin as possible. Light the candle. Cover the lit candle with the glass.

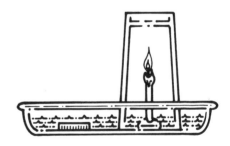

When the candle goes out (having used up all the oxygen in the glass) the water will be pushed by air pressure up into the glass (where there is a partial vacuum). The dish is now dry and you simply reach in and pick up the coin.

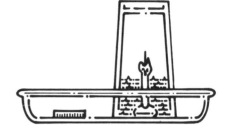

Performance tips: This effect is good for a small show. You might ask if anyone knows what makes it work. Then explain it. It's a fun science lesson.

Drag Race: Aerodynamic Action

The challenge is to drop a stamp and a fifty-cent piece at the same instant from the same height and have them reach the ground at the same time. Those who try are doomed to fail. Then you show how it's done.

WHAT'S HAPPENING

If a feather and a ball are dropped at the same instant from the same height on the moon, they both reach the ground at the same time. On earth it's another story. The feather flutters and weaves on its journey to the ground, arriving much later than the ball, which quickly travels straight down. The difference in performance between earth and moon is due to the presence of air on earth. On the moon there is a nearly perfect vacuum.

Every object moving through air sets up a disturbance called *turbulence*. If there is enough turbulence the flight of the object is unsteady. Air also exerts friction on objects moving through it. This force is called air resistance or *drag*. The amount of drag on an object and the steadiness of its flight depend on the shape of the object and its speed. Streamlining and smoother surfaces reduce drag and turbulence.

A postage stamp flutters slowly to the ground because drag and turbulence act against the force of gravity. Drag and turbulence also affect a falling coin. But the weight of the coin is enough so that it's hardly slowed down.

In this stunt, the coin and stamp are arranged so drag and turbulence have little effect on the stamp.

THE ACT

All you need is a fifty-cent piece and a stamp that is smaller than the coin. Pose the challenge to your audience. Can anyone drop both objects at the same time from the same height and have them reach the ground at the same time? Most people will hold the stamp in one hand and the coin in the other. The coin will always reach the ground first.

After a few people have tried and failed, you show your audience how to do it. Place the stamp on top of the coin, making sure there are no corners sticking out over the edge. Press the stamp down to make sure there is as much contact between the two surfaces as possible. The idea is to keep air from moving under the stamp and lifting it from the coin. Drop the coin and stamp together as shown in the picture. The coin shields the stamp from the effects of motion through air.

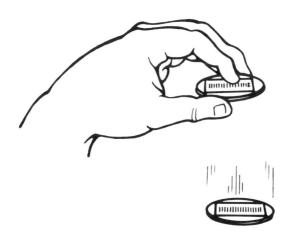

Performance tips: This is an entertaining stunt for a party or get-together. Ask your friends if they know why your method of dropping the coin works.

Leakproof Sieve: A Study of Surface Tension

You pour water through a tea strainer so no one can doubt the strainer is full of holes. Then you show how it holds water without spilling a drop. Suddenly either the sieve is leakproof or you've found an invisible lining.

WHAT'S HAPPENING

Water, like other matter, exists in three states: solid, gas, and liquid. The molecules of which water is made interact with one another, and the type of interaction between molecules is different in different states.

When water is ice (solid), the molecules are in fixed positions, vibrating in place. They are strongly attracted to one another. When water is steam (gas), the molecules move freely, sometimes colliding with one another. The attraction between molecules in the gas state is very small because there are great distances between them. When water is a liquid, the molecules move past one another. They are close enough to be strongly attracted to one another but are moving too quickly to be held in a fixed position.

The attraction between the molecules of liquid water is strongest at the surface where air and water meet. Water molecules are more attracted to one another than they are to air molecules. They pull together at the boundary between air and water to form an invisible "skin." This pulling together of the molecules is called *surface tension*.

Surface tension can be strong enough to keep liquid water inside a container full of holes.

THE SETUP

> white paraffin (the kind used to seal jelly jars)
> an aluminum pan
> a wire tea strainer

Following the directions on the package, melt the paraffin in the pan over a low flame. Dip the strainer into the melted wax. As you remove the strainer, give it a hard shake over the pan while the paraffin is still hot. The idea is to coat the wires of the strainer lightly with wax but still keep it full of holes.

THE ACT

> Have on a table:
> the waxed tea strainer

a pitcher of water

a basin

a small square of plastic wrap that neatly fits into the
   tea strainer

Demonstrate that the strainer is full of holes by
pouring water through it into the basin. The weight of
the falling water will force it through the coated holes.

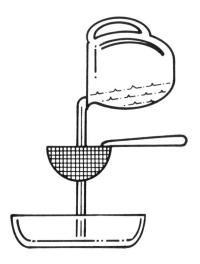

Then slip the small square of plastic wrap into the
strainer as you announce that your magic can keep
water in the strainer despite the holes. If anyone com-
ments on the plastic wrap, carry on as if you didn't
hear. Let people think you are very bad at making con-
cealed motions.

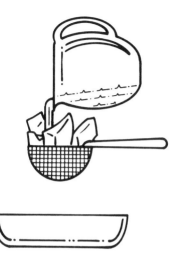

Pour water into the plastic-lined strainer. Finally, after enough people have remarked on the plastic, say, "Oh, you think this plastic keeps the water in?" Slide the plastic out and the water remains in the strainer!

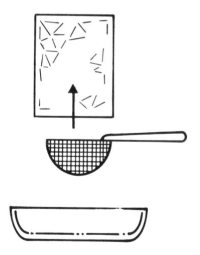

Here's how this trick works: Surface tension is not a very strong force. Water molecules often come in contact with materials that attract them more than they are attracted to one another. When water is attracted to another surface, that surface becomes wet. Water will, for example, wet the wires of a strainer. But paraffin and water are hardly attracted to each other. Water rolls off a waxed surface, keeping its own surface tension. By coating the wires with wax, you prevent the wires from becoming wet and decreasing the surface tension of the water.

The force of falling water is enough to cause water to pass through the waxed holes. You need the piece of plastic to break the force of the falling water when you pour. But when you remove the plastic, the surface tension of the water between the wires is strong enough to keep the rest of the water in the strainer.

Performance tips: This is an effective trick for a small audience. Since your props are small your audience should have a fairly close view. On the other hand, you don't want anyone close enough to detect the way you've "doctored" the strainer.

Acting Like Moses: Breaking Surface Tension

Moses raised his hands and the Red Sea waters rushed away. You too can make red waters part, leaving a dry spot behind. Behold!

WHAT'S HAPPENING

Different liquids have different surface tensions. You can see this if you put drops of water, salad oil, rubbing alcohol, and turpentine on a sheet of waxed paper. Compare the shapes of the drops by looking at them sideways. The drop with the highest and roundest shape has the most surface tension, while the flattest drop has the least.

When liquids with different surface tensions come in contact with each other there is a lot of motion. The two liquids will pull in opposite directions, and the liquid with the stronger surface tension will pull harder. If the pull is strong enough and the depth of the liquid is very shallow, such a tug-of-war between two liquids can leave a dry spot.

water
a small flat plate (preferably light in color)
red food coloring
a straw or medicine dropper
a small bottle of rubbing alcohol that can be dis-
guised as containing a "magic fluid"

Pour a thin layer of water into the plate as you
talk about the way Moses parted the Red Sea so his
people could escape the Egyptian soldiers. Add a few
drops of red food coloring to make the water more like
the Red Sea.

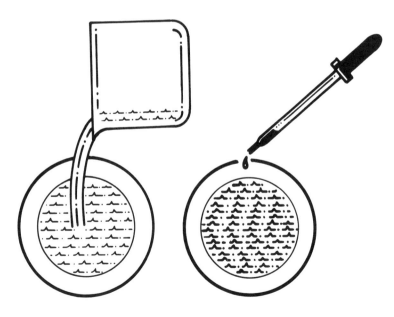

Now explain that you have a magic fluid that can do what Moses did. Put the straw into the bottle of alcohol. The alcohol will quickly rise in the straw. This is because the alcohol molecules are attracted to the sides of the straw. Put your finger over the open top of the straw so the alcohol remains inside. Place the end of the straw over the center of the red water. Lift your finger off the top of the straw, and the alcohol will run out onto the plate. When it hits the surface the red water rushes away, leaving a dry spot where you

put the alcohol. This happens because the surface tension of alcohol is less than the surface tension of water. The water pulls away on all sides from the alcohol, leaving a dry spot behind.

Performance tips: This trick has to be viewed close-up, so your audience can see the small but dramatic effect.

The Intelligent Eggs: Buoyancy

You give two eggs to a member of your audience. Ask a volunteer to write the word "sink" on one and "float" on the other. You then place each egg in a glass of water and order them to obey the commands written on them. Naturally, they're smart enough to do as they are told.

WHAT'S HAPPENING

When you put a body (such as your own) in water, here's what happens: Water is pushed aside as the object takes up space that had been occupied by the water. And if you could somehow attach a scale to the object, you'd find it weighed less in water than it weighed on dry land. You'd also find that a floating body gave a zero reading on a scale. Water exerts an upward force, called *buoyancy*, that works against the downward force of gravity, or weight.

Over two thousand years ago, a Greek named Archimedes investigated buoyancy. He submerged objects in a container that was filled to the brim with water and collected all the water that overflowed. He discovered that the liquid he collected took up the same amount of space as the submerged object. Then he weighed the overflow. He found that the weight of the displaced water exactly equaled the weight lost by the object when it was submerged. If the object floated, the weight of the displaced water equaled the weight of the object in air.

Archimedes also found that some liquids have greater buoyancy than others. If you took the same volumes of fresh water and water containing dissolved material, such as salt or sugar, you'd find the fresh water weighs less than the solution. Since salt or sugar water weighs more than an equal volume of fresh water, it has greater buoyancy. In other words, it can push up with greater force. If you've gone swimming in both salt and fresh water, you've probably noticed that you float more easily in salt water.

The eggs appear to obey written commands, but the trick here lies in the "water" in the glasses.

THE SETUP

 two 8-ounce glasses
 water
 four tablespoons sugar
 two uncooked eggs
 laundry marking pencil

Well before performance time, fill the glasses with water to about three-fourths inch below the top. Dissolve four tablespoons of sugar in one glass. Be sure to remember by position which glass is which.

THE ACT

Announce you have two intelligent eggs that obey written commands. Give them to a member of your audience with a marking pencil and give him or her the choice as to which egg will have the word "sink" and which will have the word "float."

water   sugar water

When the marked eggs are returned to you, put the egg marked "sink" in the glass with plain water and the "float" egg in the sugar water. The sugar water

water   sugar water

has enough buoyancy so that the egg will float. Afterward you can break open the eggs to show there is no trick inside.

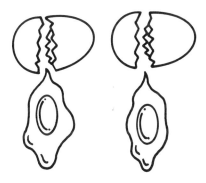

Performance tips: This trick uses an old standby of magicians called "misdirection." You call attention to the eggs, making it appear that any difference in behavior is due to them. This diverts people's attention away from where the real secret of the trick lies. The more you draw people's attention to possible differences between the eggs, the less likely they are to think that there is a difference in the contents of the glasses.

This is an effective trick for a small magic show.

The Rising Raisins: Buoyancy & Surface Tension

Drop a few raisins in some ginger ale and they quickly sink to the bottom of the glass. But, at the sound of your masterful voice, some rise to the surface, only to fall back again at your command. Directions for training raisins follow.

WHAT'S HAPPENING

There are several things going on here. Soda contains carbon dioxide gas, which collects as bubbles that rise to the surface. Gas bubbles rise because the buoyant force of the soda water is greater than the weight of the bubbles. The rough surface of a raisin provides many points of attachment for bubbles of gas. As bubbles collect on a raisin's surface, it becomes more and more buoyant until it finally rises to the surface of the ginger ale.

The gas inside the bubble expands as the bubble

rises to the surface and the pressure on it lessens. When the bubble reaches the surface, it expands even more. The thin film of liquid surrounding it is stretched too thin to hold the gas inside, and the bubble breaks, releasing the gas to the air. (The ginger ale in the film collects into a droplet when the bubble breaks.) With the loss of support from the gas bubbles, the raisin sinks to the bottom, where it remains until a new batch of bubbles collects on its surface.

THE SETUP & THE ACT

    a few raisins
    a glass of fresh ginger ale or other light-colored soda

Drop a few raisins into the soda. Mention that some

raisins

fresh ginger ale

raisins are more obedient than others. Watch carefully as bubbles collect. It will only take a few seconds for the raisins to start to rise. As soon as you see one of the raisins beginning to move, command it to rise. When it reaches the surface, tell it to fall.

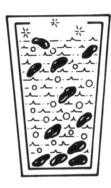

Performance tips: This trick has to be seen close up. It's most effective if done when you're sitting around with a few friends, having a snack. If you handle the act smoothly, many people will not realize that your command has nothing to do with the rise and fall of the raisins.

Diving Baby:
Hydraulic Pressure & Buoyancy

With a flourish you bring forward a tiny doll floating in a baby bottle full of water. The doll sinks and rises according to directions from your audience.

WHAT'S HAPPENING

The secret behind this trick is the difference in the behavior of a liquid and a gas when a force is applied to them. When pressure is applied to a gas (in this case air), it is squeezed into a smaller space. Liquids (in this case water), cannot be squeezed anywhere near as much. When pressure is applied to one side of a container holding a liquid, the liquid will flow into any opening or weak spot in the container. If there is no place for the liquid to go, it will push out against the container.

This trick is a variation on a classic physical phenomenon called a Cartesian diver. The doll has an air bubble in its head, which makes it buoyant enough to float just under the surface of the water in the bottle. Below the air bubble, the doll is filled with water that can flow freely in and out through a hole in the bottom of the doll's feet.

When pressure is applied to the water in the bottle, water is forced up through the hole in the doll's feet. The air bubble is squeezed into a smaller space, and the additional water inside the doll makes it less buoyant, so it sinks. When the pressure on the water is released, the air bubble springs back to its former size, pushing out the extra water, and the doll again rises to the surface.

THE SETUP

> a clear plastic baby bottle
> a blind nipple (This is a nipple which has no holes. It can be purchased at any drugstore.)
> an inexpensive, hollow plastic baby doll, small enough to fit into the bottle (You can get dolls like this in dime stores and novelty shops. The dolls are made in a single piece, without movable arms or legs.)
> a large nail
> a pair of pliers
> some small lead fishing weights
> plastic wrap

The baby doll may come wrapped in a small piece of flannel. Remove this. Use the nail to make a hole in the feet of the doll. (WARNING: You will be using the stove to heat the nail. So check with an adult before you begin.) Hold the head end of the nail with the pliers. Heat the other end over a burner of the

stove. Press the hot point of the nail into the bottom of the doll's feet. Make a hole just large enough to insert two or three small lead fishing weights.

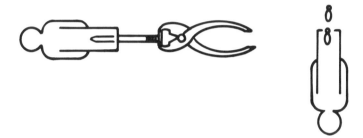

It takes a bit of fussing to get the doll diver to work properly. Put a small amount of water in the doll. Drop

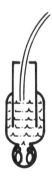

it, feet first, into a full bottle of water. The doll should rise and come to rest with its head just barely under

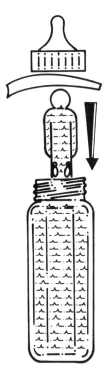

water. If the doll remains near the bottom of the bottle, remove it and shake out some of the water. If the doll floats above the surface, remove it and add a little water.

When the doll is resting in the proper position, place a small piece of plastic wrap over the mouth of the bottle and screw on the top with the blind nipple. It's important that you make the seal airtight. You may find that the doll sinks a bit when you screw on the top. If this happens, you have to take the whole thing apart and remove some of the water from the doll. It should maintain the proper position with the top in place. Check to make sure it's working properly by squeezing the sides of the bottle. Very slight pressure on the sides of the bottle should be enough to cause the doll to sink.

THE ACT

Present your baby diver by holding the bottle in your hand. The audience should be able to see the doll easily. You can have your audience command the doll to sink and rise. Squeeze the sides gently to make it sink and release the pressure to make it rise. No one should be able to detect the small motion of your hand.

Performance tips: You might want to pass the bottle around so others can try to make the doll sink and rise. You may wish to explain the science behind the effect.

4
Energy Enchantments

The universe consists of matter and energy. We may learn of the existence of energy by observing what it does to matter. One thing energy does is make matter move. Energy has an effect on the matter of which we are made. Without it we could not see, or hear, or respond to our environment.

There are different kinds of energy. Heat, light, electricity, and motion are some of the forms energy takes. One kind of energy can change into another. Rub your hands together quickly for a demonstration of how motion can become heat. In a light bulb electricity becomes heat in a wire; the heat then becomes light as the wire glows white-hot. Power plants change the motion of falling water into electricity for millions of homes. Heat energy from burning gasoline becomes motion in automobiles and trucks.

This chapter will introduce you to some of the different forms energy takes. The tricks will give you a small sampling of some of the properties of different types of energy.

The Writhing Snake: Kinetic & Potential Energy

From your pocket you produce a small coiled snake that twists and writhes as if it's alive.

WHAT'S HAPPENING

Everything that moves has energy of motion or *kinetic* energy. The kinetic energy of an object may be due to a push, or a pull, or an explosion. Sometimes something happens to an object so that energy is stored and can become kinetic energy at some later time. A spring can be wound very tightly. It can stay in this condition until it is released. An object that has stored energy (such as a coiled spring) has *potential* energy.

In this trick you can see how kinetic energy becomes potential energy that is released in a different form of kinetic energy. The motion of your hands (kinetic energy) is used to wind up something like a spring

that remains coiled (potential energy) until you release it (kinetic energy again).

a 4-inch piece of stretchable plastic wrap
a paper clip

Hold one corner of the plastic wrap in one hand.
Twist the wrap with the other hand by making circular
motions with one finger. Continue until the plastic
wrap is *very* tightly wound in a rope shape. Then

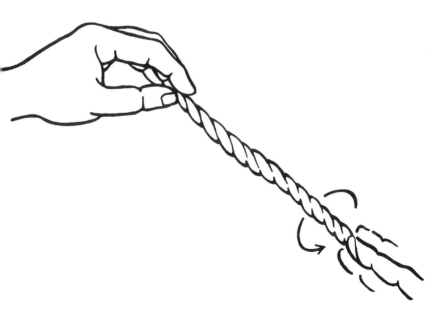

coil it so it is flat and round. Make a small knot at one end (being careful not to let it unwind). The knot can be the snake's head. Hold the coil in position with a paper clip and keep it out of sight in a pocket or bag until you are ready to perform.

THE ACT

Announce you have a live act as you reach into your pocket or bag. Remove the paper clip while your hand is still hidden from sight, holding the snake so it doesn't unwind. Let the clip drop to the bottom of your pocket or bag. Bring out the coiled snake and release it.

Performance tips: This trick is amusing for a close-up audience, especially one with very young children. You might want to show them how they can make their own "snakes." To get the most out of the act, you should try to surprise your audience by quickly producing the moving snake.

The Devil's Handkerchief: Heat Conduction

You hold the red-hot end of a glowing piece of wood against a handkerchief for fifteen seconds. Amazingly, the handkerchief isn't scorched.

WHAT'S HAPPENING

Fire is a release of heat and light energy as fuel combines with oxygen in a chemical reaction. (More about chemical reactions in the next chapter.) In addition to fuel and oxygen, a source of heat is essential for burning to occur.

Some fuels need very little heat to get started burning. The chemicals on a match head ignite from the tiny amount of heat generated by friction when the match is struck. Paper and cloth start burning at higher temperatures. Cloth will burn through when exposed to the heat of a piece of hot glowing wood.

In this trick, you prevent the cloth from scorching upon exposure to glowing wood by removing the heat from the cloth before it gets hot enough to burn. The heat of the glowing wood passes through the cloth into a substance called a *heat conductor* that gets hot very quickly and easily without itself burning. Heat travels through the conductor, so it leaves the area being heated and the temperature of the cloth cannot build to a point where it would burn. Metals are good heat conductors, and of the metals silver is one of the best.

THE SETUP & THE ACT

> a handkerchief (or a clean piece of old sheet)
> a quarter
> a candle
> matches
> a pencil or a small piece of wooden dowel (We used the handle of a paintbrush.)

Wrap the handkerchief around the quarter, twist-

ing it behind the coin to make a flat surface. Set the coin and handkerchief aside. Light the candle. Put one end of the pencil or wooden dowel in the flame and keep it there until at least a quarter of an inch is glowing red-hot. Hold the glowing end of the wood against the cloth lying on top of the coin for about fifteen seconds. Remove the glowing wood and you'll find there is no trace of scorched fabric.

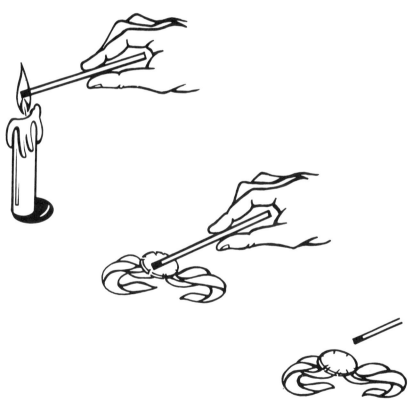

The quarter is a good conductor of heat because it contains silver. If you feel the coin immediately following the removal of the heat source it will be warm. And what is more, the heat will be evenly distributed through the coin. The part that had been directly under the glowing wood will not be any warmer than the rest of the coin.

Performance tips: This effect has to be viewed close up. If you would like to turn it into a science experiment (and don't mind burning a hole in the fabric), try the procedure again without the coin. It will only take about fifteen seconds to burn a hole in the cloth.

A Stamped-Out Stamp: Light Refraction

You place a perfectly transparent object over a stamp and the stamp disappears! "Light action" is the name for this stamp act.

WHAT'S HAPPENING

Light is a form of energy that travels at very high speeds. It can pass through space and through air, water, glass, and many other materials. In order to see an object, light from that object must reach your eyes. This means the object must itself be a source of light, or it must reflect light (bounce light off it) to your eyes. Some materials are transparent (which means you can see through them, as if they weren't there) because light passes through them.

When a beam of light passes at an angle from one transparent material to another, the beam is usually bent (refracted) at the boundary. In this trick a stamp is covered with a jar filled with water. The cover on the jar prevents you from looking directly down on the stamp and you must look at it at an angle through the side of the jar. As light from the stamp passes from the water to air, it is bent in such a way that the stamp looks like it's higher than it really is. If you fill the jar with water, light from the stamp doesn't reach your eyes, so the stamp is impossible to see.

THE SETUP & THE ACT

an empty peanut butter jar and cover
a stamp

You can paint and decorate the cover of the jar with nail polish, if you wish. Fill the jar with water and cover it.

Show your audience the covered jar, pointing out that it is transparent and one can see through it perfectly. Place the jar over the stamp. If it is correctly placed, no one can see the stamp from any angle around the jar. Remove the jar and the stamp reappears.

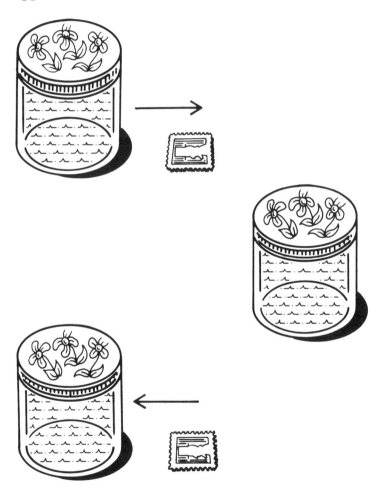

Performance tips: This is a close-up effect. You must be careful to fill the jar, because if the jar is less than full, the stamp will appear to be inside the jar.

VARIETY ACT

A curved transparent object can act as a lens and refract light so as to completely reverse an image. The picture shows how this happens. Place a card with an arrow drawn on it behind your water-filled peanut butter jar. When you view it from the front, the direction of the arrow will be reversed. You will have to experiment to see how far behind the jar you must place the card to get the proper effect.

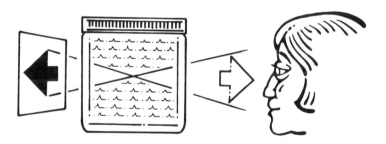

The Phantom Memory: Phosphorescence

A friend selects a number on a chart by covering it with a small piece of cardboard. This move is unseen by you. Yet you can tell where the cardboard rested.

WHAT'S HAPPENING

There are certain minerals that have an unusual ability. They absorb light energy. Later, the light energy is released as a ghostly green light which can be seen in the dark. This phenomenon is called *phosphorescence*. The brightness of the glow depends on the amount of light the phosphorescent material has been exposed to. If there has been a long exposure to bright light, the material will glow more brightly in the dark than when there has been a shorter exposure.

You can take advantage of this phenomenon in performing the next trick.

THE SETUP

phosphorescent tape (This is sometimes called "luminous" tape. You can buy it in any photography store. It's used in darkrooms to mark light switches, etc.)

colored paper

marking pen

scissors

a small piece of cardboard

a dark scarf or a large piece of dark cloth

pencil and paper

Put several strips of tape on colored paper and mark the paper off in numbered squares as shown in the picture. Outline the squares in ink. Cut out a piece of cardboard to exactly fit one square. To perform, you'll need the chart, the cardboard, the scarf, and the pencil and paper.

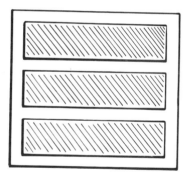

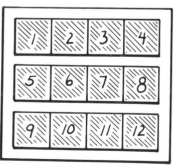

This trick should be performed in a brightly lit room. A tabletop with a lamp on it is a good place on which to rest the number chart.

Place the dark scarf over your head so it covers your face. With your back turned, ask a friend to select a number by covering it with the cardboard square. Your friend is, of course, to keep his or her choice a secret from you.

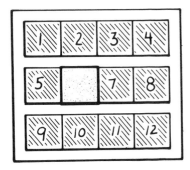

To stall for time, ask your friend to do some mathematical operations with this number. The pencil and paper are for figuring. You might ask that the number be multiplied by five, that the year of your friend's birth be added, and today's date subtracted. Most people won't realize that this is a lot of nonsense.

Ask for the solution, have the scratch paper torn up, and have the cardboard square removed. Point out that there is no evidence to give you a clue to the selected number. Pick up the chart, turn your back again, and bring the chart up under the scarf. (You can claim to be tuning in your thought waves.) In the dim light under the scarf you'll see that the square which was covered will be much dimmer than the other squares. Announce the correct number with a flourish.

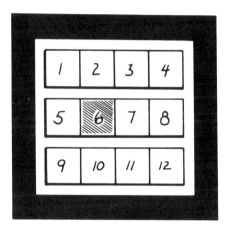

Performance tips: This is a good trick for a show with a small audience so everyone can get a close-up look at the chart. You can repeat this trick, if you wish. The second time use your creativity and have an entirely different set of mathematical operations performed on the number.

A Song & Dance Act: Sympathetic Vibrations

You run your finger around the rim of a crystal goblet, making it sing. Meanwhile, a wire on a nearby goblet dances.

WHAT'S HAPPENING

Pluck a stretched rubber band, strike a bell, or draw a bow across a violin string, and you produce a rapid back and forth motion in these objects called *vibration*. Vibrating objects set up waves in air known as sound waves. The varieties of sounds you hear are due to the many different ways objects vibrate.

If you wet your finger and run it around the rim of a crystal goblet, you'll set up vibrations you'll hear as a pure tone, which is the simplest kind of sound energy. The highness or lowness of the tone depends on the number of vibrations per second, which is called the *natural frequency* of the goblet. If a nearby object is tuned to the same natural frequency as the tone, it will respond by vibrating when the tone is produced. Sometimes such *sympathetic vibrations* can be so strong that the object breaks. An example is the breaking of a mirror or glass by an opera singer's voice.

In this trick, the vibrations of one goblet set up

vibrations in another one nearby. There is little chance of breaking the second glass, however, as the tone produced by the first glass will not be strong enough.

THE SETUP

    two identical crystal goblets with stems
    an unbent paper clip or hairpin
    water

This setup takes a bit of fussing and practice before you'll be ready to perform. First practice making a goblet sing. The glass and your finger should be clean and free of grease. Moisten the forefinger of your right hand. Hold the glass in place with your left hand on the base as you rotate your wet finger around the rim.

You'll soon learn just how much pressure to apply to produce a steady ringing tone.

The next problem is to get both goblets to produce the same tone. To tune the goblets, tap the sides, first of one, then of the other, with a wooden pencil or the back of a wooden spoon. This lets you test the tone. Add a small amount of water to each goblet until they produce the same note. Adding water lowers the tone and removing it raises the tone. The trick will not work if the goblets are not properly tuned.

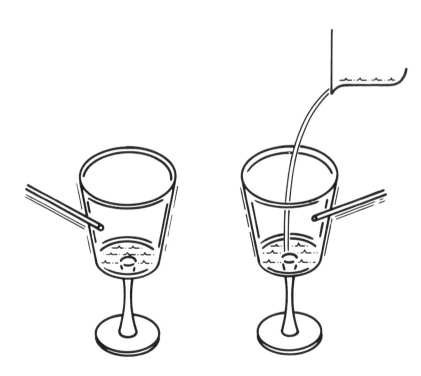

THE ACT

Announce that two friendly glasses will perform a song and dance act. The goblets should be side by side about two inches apart. The wire hairpin or opened paper clip should be lying across the rim of one goblet. Run your wet finger around the rim of the other goblet, making it sing. Its tone will set up sympathetic vibrations in the other goblet, causing the wire to move around on the rim.

Performance tips: This effect is best performed informally, for instance after dinner. Your friends may be interested in an explanation of the science behind the phenomenon.

The Wondrous Wand: Electrostatics

With a wave of your wand you make paper dance, move a plastic bubble, and wiggle some toothpicks. Both you and your audience can get a charge from this.

WHAT'S HAPPENING

Thousands of years ago the Greeks knew of a "magic" stone—a kind of petrified pine resin known today as amber. When amber is rubbed with fur, it gets a strange temporary power. Nearby bits of paper and cork move toward the stone and stick to it. The Greek name for amber is *elektros*. Today this power of attraction is called electrostatic attraction.

You can produce electrostatic attraction in many modern nonmetal materials by rubbing them with other materials. Rub a balloon against a wool sleeve, rub rubber soles against a rug, brush your hair on a dry day. Friction gives these objects an electric *charge*, which gives them the power to attract other objects. Charged objects act similarly to magnets for a short time until they lose their charge to the air or the objects they touch. In this trick you give an electric charge to a plastic wand.

THE SETUP

> a plastic rod or tube for a wand (We used the handle of a plastic flyswatter.)
> a wool scarf (or a scarf made of synthetic fibers)
> various items to be "electrified" such as: plastic tinsel, plastic bubbles (the kind you blow on the end of a straw from liquid that comes in a tube), wooden toothpicks, paper cutouts of people made of tissue paper and placed in a glass dish covered with plastic wrap

Have everything ready before you perform.

THE ACT

It's better if you perform this trick on a dry day, as moisture in the air prevents a good charge from building up.

Show your friends your "magic" wand. Rub it well with the cloth. Wave the charged wand near the

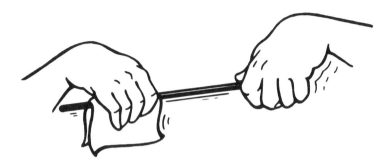

objects to be "electrified." The objects will move as the wand comes near them. Rub the wand whenever you find it needs recharging.

Performance tips: This is a very familiar phenomenon but your friends may not know why it happens. Experiment to see what effect the charged wand has when you bring it near another object and when you touch it to that object.

VARIETY ACTS

Charge yourself by walking across a woolen rug while wearing rubber-soled shoes. You'll find the charge is in your hands and you can transfer it to playing cards you hold in your hands. If you slap the charged playing cards against the wall, electrostatic attraction will hold them up.

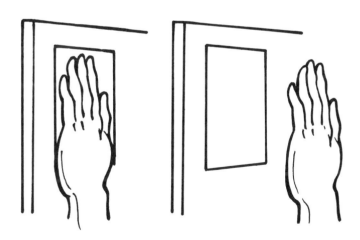

You can use electrostatic attraction to hold a sheet of newspaper up against a wall. Open a single sheet, put it against the wall, and rub it with a woolen cloth. When you take the cloth away, the newspaper will cling to the wall.

5

Chemical Conjuring

Of all the people who played around with natural events, perhaps none seemed more like magicians than the alchemists. They labored among their caldrons and flasks during the Middle Ages, like mysterious chefs, cooking up recipes to change one substance into another. They mixed, and heated, and separated, and mixed in countless combinations and recombinations.

The push behind their hot and sweaty labor was the goal of changing ordinary materials into gold. Always they failed in their purpose. But no matter what their motive, they did discover a great deal of practical information about the stuff of which the earth is made, information which became the groundwork of the science of chemistry. Unfortunately, it took a long time for the discoveries of alchemists to become public knowledge. They were very secretive about their procedures, always afraid someone else might use them to win the race to wealth.

Modern chemistry is the science that deals with the properties of materials and how materials can be transformed. The basic materials on earth are called *elements*, of which gold is one. Substances made of combinations of elements can be transformed through many of the procedures alchemists discovered into substances with very different properties. But one element cannot be used to make another with ordinary kinds of chemical procedures.

The tricks in this chapter demonstrate different kinds of chemical transformations. Conjure up a few and you'll see how the alchemists got hooked.

The Flying Flame: Introducing a Chemical Reaction

You make a flame jump from one candle to another. And, in a variety act, you separate a flame from a candle, so it burns a few inches *above* the wick.

WHAT'S HAPPENING

Materials with one set of properties transform into substances with another set of properties by going through a *chemical reaction.* The lightweight metal sodium combines with poisonous, yellow chlorine gas to form sodium chloride, which you know as table salt. Oxygen and hydrogen gases react with each other to form water. One of the most familiar chemical reactions occurs when a candle burns. Candle wax reacts with oxygen in the air to form water vapor and carbon dioxide. The products of chemical reactions often have very different properties from the starting materials.

All chemical reactions involve energy. In the case of the burning candle, heat energy and light energy, which you see as a flame, are given off during the reaction. The match needed to ignite the candle supplies enough energy to make the wax hot enough to combine with oxygen. After that, the heat given off in the reaction is enough to keep it going so additional wax reacts.

When you blow out a candle, some of the hot wax leaves the wick as smoke. This wax vapor is hot enough to burn if you bring a flame close to it. In this stunt, a flame travels down a column of hot wax vapor to reignite the wick from which the vapor comes. It appears as if the flame is jumping through the air.

THE SETUP & THE ACT

    waxed paper
    two candles
    matches

111

Spread the waxed paper on the table to catch candle wax as it drips. Light both candles, announcing that you have the power to make a flame jump from one to the other. You might want to invent a story around this idea; for instance, talk about flame throwing being an art of the devil.

Hold a candle in each hand. When the flames are burning strongly, turn the candles sideways so they are burning near each other. Blow out the flame of one candle and move it an inch or two below the other, still burning, candle. The column of smoke from the unlit candle should rise to meet the flame. The reac-

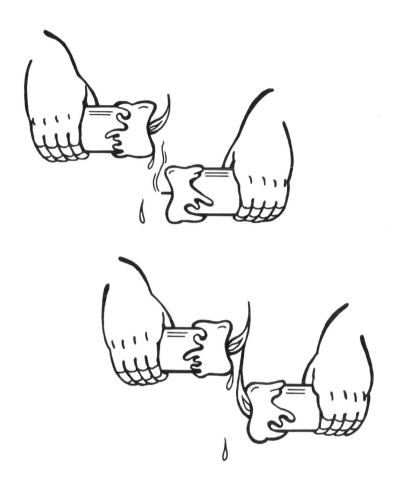

tion quickly travels down the smoke, causing the wick to reignite. Fire appears to jump through the air.

Performance tips: This effect has to be viewed close up, as the distance you can hold the candles apart is small.

You will first have to make a jar of carbon dioxide. Put about two tablespoons of vinegar and one tablespoon of baking soda in the bottom of a jar. The bubbles that form hold carbon dioxide, one of the products of a chemical reaction between vinegar and baking soda. Carbon dioxide gas is heavier than air and as it evolves (as it is produced) it drives air from the jar. After a while you can cover the jar to prevent the invisible gas from spilling over the edge. It will, however, remain in an uncovered jar for at least a half hour. (You can also make a jar of carbon dioxide according to the procedure described on pp. 117–119.)

You will need:

a short candle in a wire holder (see illustration)
matches

Light the candle. When it is burning strongly, lower it carefully by the wire holder into the jar of carbon

dioxide. The flame will remain near the mouth of the jar while the candle wick is extinguished. It will take a bit of experimenting to see how far you can lower the candle before the flame goes out.

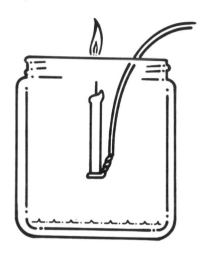

The flame separates from its wick because the end of the column of smoke burns at the invisible boundary between carbon dioxide and air. The smoke reacts with the oxygen in the air, but it will not react with the carbon dioxide in the jar.

Performance tips: This is a startling effect for close-up viewing. Ask your friends if they can explain the phenomenon, but don't tell anyone that there is something besides air in the jar until after they've tried to figure it out.

The Spirited Fire Extinguisher: Carbon Dioxide in Action

You pick up an empty jar, pour its invisible contents over a candle, and the flame goes out! Are you pouring it on or putting it on? Let them wonder.

WHAT'S HAPPENING

Carbon dioxide is a colorless, odorless gas as is oxygen. Unlike oxygen, however, carbon dioxide will not react with a fuel, such as wax, and does not burn. In fact, it prevents burning and can be used to extinguish any flame in its presence. In this trick you stop an ongoing reaction by replacing one of the reacting substances (oxygen) with one that won't react.

Carbon dioxide is heavier than air. That's why you can pour it out of a jar even if you can't see it.

THE SETUP

> several jars of carbon dioxide (See the procedure for collecting carbon dioxide below.)
> candleholder with candles (You can make a long

candleholder out of clay and put in a row of ten or fifteen birthday candles.)

matches

jar with cap to use as a generating chamber

screwdriver

clay

jars with caps to hold the gas

plastic tubing (This can be obtained from a store that sells aquarium supplies.)

pan of water

bottle of club soda

bowl of warm water

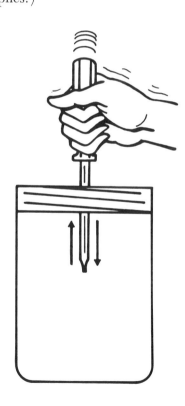

Poke a hole in the lid of a jar with the screwdriver. This jar will be used as a generating chamber.

Put one end of the plastic tubing through the hole and mold clay around it to make an airtight seal with the lid. Fill one of the jars for collecting with water. Submerge it in the pan of water and turn it upside down. Leave it sitting on the bottom. Fill the generating chamber half full of club soda. Screw on the top and pass the tube into the pan. Put the generating chamber in a bowl of warm water. As its contents heat up, carbon dioxide gas (the fizz in soda) is driven off. You'll see bubbles coming out of the end of the tube in the pan. Let the gas bubble for a few minutes to drive off the air

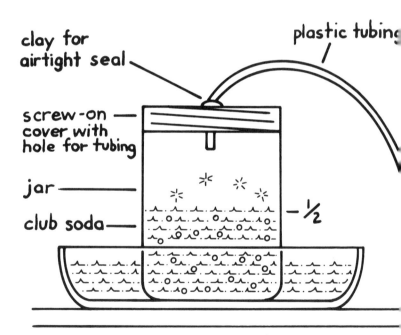

clay for airtight seal

plastic tubing

screw-on cover with hole for tubing

jar

club soda

$-\frac{1}{2}$

in the generating chamber. Then put the end of the tube in the upside-down jar in the pan.

Carbon dioxide bubbles rise and fill the jar, driving out the water. Remove a full jar of gas by sliding a plate under it when it is still in the water. After removing the jar, turn it right side up and screw on a cover until you are ready to perform.

Before performing have the jars of gas ready and have the candles and matches handy. There should be no sign of the equipment used to collect the gas.

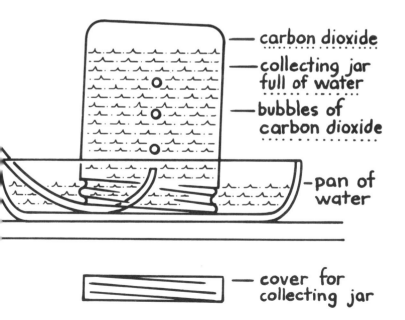

— carbon dioxide

—collecting jar full of water

—bubbles of carbon dioxide

-pan of water

— cover for collecting jar

Pass a closed jar of carbon dioxide around so all can see it is empty. (Don't let anyone open it.) Tell the audience you can put out candles with the help of a "spirit" trapped in the seemingly empty jars. Light the candles. Remove the cover of a jar and make a pouring motion over the candles. They will all go out. If people want to see the trick again, you can repeat it with another jar of gas.

Performance tips: This trick is a good one for an informal show.

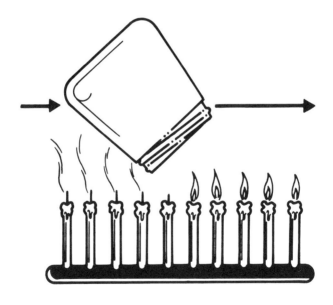

Think Milk:
Precipitation

Water changes into milk as you pour it into a glass. Thinking hard about milk did the trick.

WHAT'S HAPPENING

Many chemical reactions take place in water solutions. When a substance is in solution, its smallest particles (atoms or molecules) are separated from one another by water molecules. Molecules are much too small to see, so solutions are clear. If they are also colorless (as is the case when sugar or salt dissolves), you can't tell the difference between a solution and plain water by just looking at it.

In this trick you mix two solutions together. The reacting molecules meet and form new products, one of which won't dissolve in water. It suddenly appears as finely divided particles, called a *precipitate*, that give the mixture a milky appearance. One important way chemists know when a chemical reaction has taken place is by watching for the formation of a precipitate.

In this reaction the precipitate is sulfur—one of the 92 natural elements in the earth's crust. Chemists sometimes call this precipitate "milk of sulfur."

> photographic fixer, also known as hypo or sodium thiosulfate (You can purchase this very inexpensively at any photography store.)
> liquid bleach containing *sodium hypochlorite* (Read the label, as this is not ordinary chlorine bleach.)
> a colorless glass pitcher
> a colorless glass tumbler
> a wand to serve as a stirring rod

Mix the hypo according to the directions on the package. You can store what you don't use in a dark bottle with a cap. Put about one cup of hypo in the

pitcher and add an equal amount of water. Put a few drops of bleach on the bottom of the glass so it is unnoticeable.

Only the pitcher, glass, and wand are present for your performance.

THE ACT

Tell your audience that you have a pitcher of water. Ask them to name other drinks. Usually someone will say "milk." But if that doesn't happen, you might bring up the subject of milk by saying it is considered to be a "perfect food."

Then ask everyone to think hard about milk (or to chant "milk" over and over again) while you pour the "water" into the glass. Use the wand to stir. You might suggest that your magic caused "skim milk" to form as the fluid has a watery appearance. You could remark that some people think the butterfat in whole milk can be harmful to older people. Remove the glass after the trick is finished, since the precipitate will soon settle out.

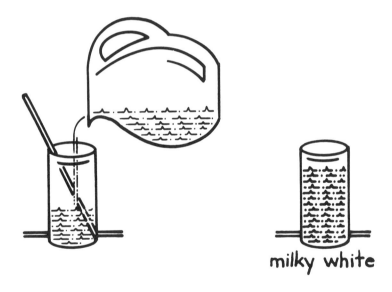

milky white

Performance tips: This is a good act for a show, but it's also fun for a small group of friends.

CAUTION: *Don't* let anyone drink the solution as it is poisonous.

The Blue Flashback: A Reversible Reaction

Pour water into a glass and it changes into ink. Pour the ink into another glass and it changes back into water. Wave your wand and it's back to ink again.

WHAT'S HAPPENING

Many chemical reactions are easily reversible. That is, reacting substances form new products which then break down to reform the original chemicals. Starch in solution is colorless and can be mixed with enough water so it looks like plain water. This small amount of starch will react with iodine to form a new substance which is blue-black and looks like ink. The starch-iodine product can be easily broken down by adding hypo. The hypo reacts with the iodine to form a product which is colorless, and the blue-black color disappears. Meanwhile, a fourth substance, hydrogen peroxide, is slowly breaking down and giving off oxygen. (You can see tiny bubbles of oxygen in a hydrogen peroxide solution if you look closely.) Oxygen reacts with hypo to form a more stable substance than the hypo-iodine material. As the hypo reacts with the oxygen, the free iodine recombines with the starch (which is still present), and the blue-black color returns. The return of color takes time because oxygen evolves slowly. The color change takes place when there is enough free iodine to react with the starch.

THE SETUP

    1 tablespoon starch solution (See the recipe below.)
    ½ cup 3 percent hydrogen peroxide (You can purchase this at any drugstore.)
    ½ cup water
    1 tablespoon white vinegar
    a few drops iodine
    one or two drops hypo (See pg. 122.)
    three clear, colorless glasses
    a wand

TO MAKE STARCH SOLUTION:

    water
    small saucepan
    1 teaspoon cornstarch
    jar with a lid

Put one cup of water in the saucepan. Add the cornstarch. Heat until the cornstarch is dissolved. Add another cup of water. Store in the jar.

This trick works best when the starch solution is fairly fresh. Put the starch solution, hydrogen peroxide, water, and vinegar in one glass. Put a few drops of iodine on the bottom of another glass. (If the glass has a thick bottom, no one will notice the iodine.) Put one or two drops of hypo on the bottom of the third glass.

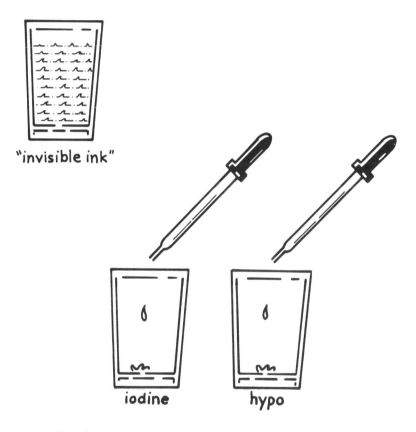

"invisible ink"

iodine   hypo

Only the three prepared glasses and the wand should be present at the performance.

A good story for this trick might be one about a secret agent who kept trying to make invisible ink that kept becoming visible.

Hold up the glass of clear liquid and call it invisible ink. Pour it into the glass containing iodine. It will turn blue-black. Then pour it into the glass containing the hypo and give the solution a stir with the wand. It will instantly become colorless again, but within fifteen seconds enough oxygen will be given off by the hydrogen peroxide to change the color back to blue-black.

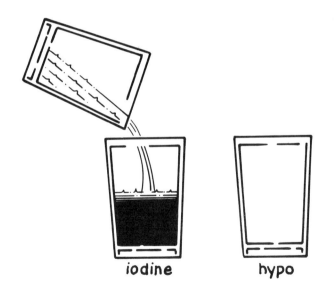

iodine   hypo

hypo

Performance tips: If you practice this trick to get the timing right, you can make it look as if a wave of your wand changed the color. This trick is good for a show.

CAUTION: *Don't* let anyone drink the solution as it is poisonous.

You can get the reaction to reverse itself again by adding additional hypo. One way to deliver a few drops of hypo without anyone noticing is to use a wand that has been dipped in hypo. You could have a spare wand that has been resting in a container with hypo.

The Purple Palette: A Chemical Indicator

You bring forth a bottle of purple paint and pour it into three glasses. It instantly changes into pink, green, and yellow paint—a magic way of creating colors.

WHAT'S HAPPENING

Color changes are one kind of sign that a chemical reaction is taking place. Certain dyes, such as litmus, change color in a reliable way when they come in contact with certain chemicals. One group of chemicals known as *acids*, which includes vinegar, lemon juice, and sulfuric acid, turns litmus from blue to pink. Another group, called *bases* or *alkalies*, which includes soap, lye, and baking soda, changes litmus from pink to blue. The color change of litmus is used in laboratories to indicate whether an unknown substance is an acid or a base.

The pigment that makes red cabbage red can be used as an indicator instead of litmus. It turns pink in acids and green in bases. Chlorine bleach will also react with it to make it colorless. The secret of this trick is the way red cabbage juice reacts with an acid, a base, and a bleach.

THE SETUP

    red cabbage juice (See procedure below.)
    white vinegar
    clear ammonia water
    chlorine bleach
    three glasses

TO PREPARE RED CABBAGE JUICE:

    red cabbage
    knife
    stainless steel or enamel pot
    strainer
    a clear, colorless pitcher or bottle

Cut up the cabbage into many fine pieces and put it in a pot with enough water to cover it. Heat until boiling. Strain the juice into a pitcher or bottle. Add water to fill the bottle if you wish. You can store red cabbage juice covered in the refrigerator for several days. It should be cool before you perform.

Before a performance put about half a teaspoon of white vinegar in one glass, half a teaspoon of ammonia water in a second glass, and half a teaspoon of bleach in a third glass. It is not likely that your audience will notice such a small amount of liquid at the bottom of each glass, but you can make certain it is unnoticeable by letting it stand or using a hair dryer until the water in each solution evaporates. The acid in the vinegar, the base in the ammonia, and the active chemical in the bleach will remain behind when the water they are dissolved in evaporates. When you add cabbage juice, the solutions reform immediately.

THE ACT

Show your audience a bottle of "paint." You might make up a story about how the purple color can be transformed into other colors if the audience chants the right magic words.

Pour the purple "paint" into each glass. In vinegar (acid) it becomes pink. In ammonia (base) it becomes bright green. In chlorine bleach it turns a faint yellow.

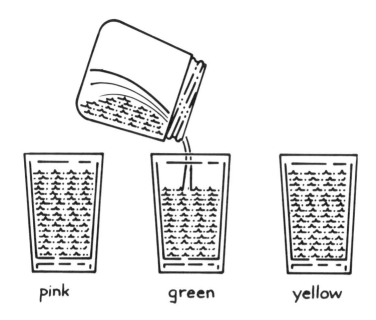

pink   green   yellow

Performance tips: This is an effective trick for a show. You can also use red cabbage juice to do science experiments and check out which kitchen chemicals are acids or bases.

CAUTION: *Do not* permit anyone to drink the contents of the glasses. Ammonia and chlorine bleach are poisonous.

6

Perceptual Puzzlements

What you see is not always what's happening. Our sense organs respond to energy and substances in the environment. Our eyes respond to light energy, our ears to sound, our skin to heat and pressure, and our tongues and noses to various chemicals. But there are limits to what our senses can perceive. X-rays are light waves that can't be seen. There are very high and very low sounds we cannot hear. And even when events are within the range of our senses, we can be fooled. If your hand is very cold and you put it in cold water, the water can feel warm. A full moon appears larger near the horizon than when it is high in the sky. Measurement of the moon has shown there is no change in the size of the moon's disk.

It's no surprise that science finally got around to

exploring the limits of human senses—after all, our senses are part of the natural world. The science of *psychophysics* investigates questions like: How dim must a light be before it can no longer be seen? How soft a sound can no longer be heard? In what ways can our senses fool us? You can have fun with some of the discoveries of psychophysics.

Our brains can play tricks on us. Sometimes we perceive things differently from the way they really are, so that it seems one thing is happening even when we know something else is really happening. A perception like this is called an illusion.

Illusions can become part of your act. We present some for your entertainment.

Quick Money: Reaction Time

You offer a dollar bill as a prize to anyone who can catch it as you let it fall. Yet time after time, it slips through grasping fingers. No one, it seems, knows how to hang on to money except you.

It takes a small amount of time—called *reaction time*—for us to respond to something we see by moving our muscles. After light from an event reaches the back of our eyes, nerves fire, carrying impulses to the brain, where connections are made with other nerves which carry impulses to our muscles. Only then do we move in response to what we see.

The time it takes to respond to the sight of the falling dollar bill is very small, less than one-fourth of a second for most people. But even though the response seems to be instantaneous, it isn't fast enough. The dollar bill falls past the grasping fingers.

This trick is so reliable that you can offer the money as a prize to anyone who catches it. Have confidence in your offer. It makes a good show and you won't be poorer for it.

THE SETUP & THE ACT

All you need for this trick is a fairly new and un-wrinkled dollar bill. (If you use a five, the trick is even more impressive.)

Announce to your audience that anyone who catches the bill when you let it drop can keep it. Hold the bill vertically by one end. Have a friend put his or her fingers around the bill. Tell the audience this is so your friend will be as "ready as possible" to grab the money as it moves past. Your friend is not to touch the bill until after you let go.

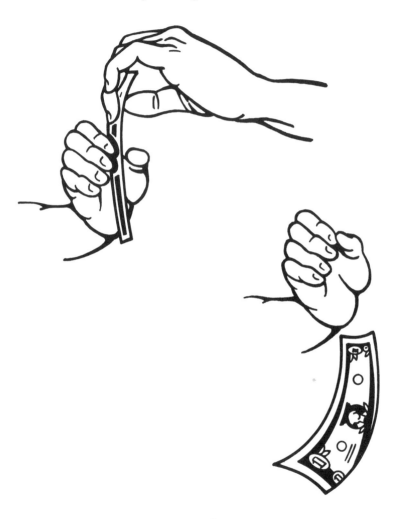

Others may want to try after the first person fails. You won't lose the money as long as you follow this procedure. The money always falls past the grasping fingers.

If you hold the bill for yourself, you'll find you will catch the bill. That's because you are not responding to the sight of the falling bill but to the feeling of letting go with one hand. This gives you just enough extra time in which to react so you can catch the bill.

Performance tips: This is fun for a party or an informal moment.

Matter Through Matter: A Motion Illusion

With a flick of your finger you make a stick move through a steel bar. There's more to this than meets the eye.

WHAT'S HAPPENING

There are several things that contribute to this trick. First, the human eye is incapable of seeing an object which is moving extremely fast. The blades of a fan can not be seen when the speed picks up.

Secondly, if the eye receives slightly different images of an object within a small fraction of a second, there is an illusion of motion. This is the principle behind motion pictures. You see one still image after another in rapid order, each slightly different from the one before, and people appear to move.

The third thing that makes this trick work is that viewers have experience with the hand movement that sets the stick in motion. They know from experience how the stick *should* move as a result of your hand motion, and most people will not realize that your hand can produce a different kind of motion in the stick.

THE SETUP & THE ACT

 a large safety pin
 a 2½-inch stick of wood or plastic (If you use a wooden match, cut off the head.)

Insert the pin through the exact center of the stick. Move the stick over to the center of the shaft of the pin. Wiggle the stick around so it moves fairly freely but will hold its position when you stop moving it.

To create the illusion: Hold the head of the pin in your left hand. Turn the stick so the top is behind the top shaft of the pin. The stick is rotating on the bottom shaft of the pin. Bring the forefinger of your right hand down hard on the bottom end of the stick. The

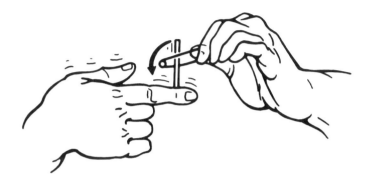

top end will appear to move forward, toward you, through the top shaft of the pin. Reset the stick to repeat the illusion.

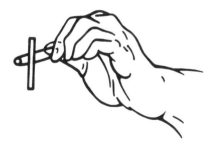

What actually happens is that the stick moves forward against the top shaft and bounces off. It is the *bottom* end of the stick that winds up in front of the top shaft of the pin. The illusion is perfect because the motion of the stick is too fast to be seen. The viewer sees two images, one behind and one in front of the top shaft of the pin. Since your viewers believe the downward motion of your finger should cause the top of the stick to move forward, they think that's what's happened, and so it seems that the stick has gone through the pin.

Performance tips: This trick has to be seen close up.

Benham's Top: A Color Illusion

You present a disk with a black and white design. Spin it and colors appear! Stop the spin and it's the same old black and white.

WHAT'S HAPPENING

Light is the form of energy to which the eye is sensitive. There is visible light. And there is light you cannot see, such as ultraviolet light and X-rays. When visible light is bright enough, as it is during the daytime or when a lamp is turned on, we can see colors as well as black and white.

After visible light enters your eye, it passes through the eyeball to the back, where it strikes an area called the *retina*. The retina is packed with special light-sensitive cells.

Nerves connected to the light-sensitive cells fire in patterns that tell your brain what you are seeing. If the retina receives repeated flashes of white light for a short time, these nerves will fire in patterns your brain interprets as color. That is, you will see color when no color really exists.

In this trick the repeated flashes of light are produced by spinning a black and white disk. This phenomenon was discovered in the nineteenth century by a man named Benham who invented a black and white top. It was a very popular toy for a while.

No one really understands why Benham's top produces the sensation of color, although there are several unproved theories.

THE SETUP

    7-inch white paper plates
    a pin
    scissors
    a ruler
    India ink and a pointed paintbrush

a phonograph turntable or a pencil with a point or a
knitting needle

The first problem is to find the exact center of a
plate. Fold a paper plate exactly in half. Open it and
fold it in half again in a different direction. The point
where the two creases cross is the center of the plate.

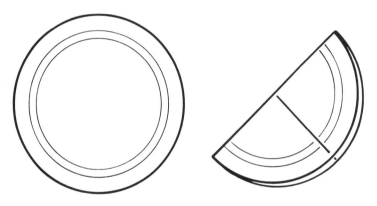

Stick a pin through at this point and lay this plate on
top of an uncreased plate. Use the pin to mark the
center.

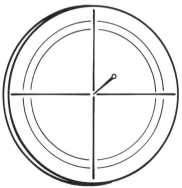

Trim the border from the uncreased plate. Using a

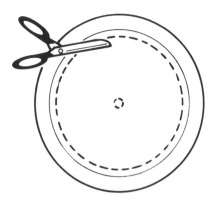

ruler and India ink (you want the black to be very black), copy one of the black and white patterns shown in the illustration. You might want to try both patterns to see which works best for you. Enlarge the

central hole so the disk fits on a phonograph turntable or will spin on a pencil point.

Show the black and white disk to your audience.
Ask if anyone sees any colors on it. Then place it on a
turntable under good lighting. It should rotate slowly.
(You might find you get a better effect if you spin it
by hand.) Instruct everyone to watch the disk and let
you know when they start seeing colors and what
colors they see.

Stop the turntable and point out that the disk is
still only black and white.

Performance tips: This is most effective as a close-up trick with a few friends.

You might want to investigate this illusion as a science project. Find out which speeds of rotation produce the illusion, how varying the amounts of black and white affects the colors people see, and if different people see different colors.

The Possessed Pendulum: A Depth Illusion

A pendulum known to be swinging from side to side can appear to be swinging in a circular path, sometimes clockwise and sometimes counterclockwise. The illusion is in the eyes of the beholder.

WHAT'S HAPPENING

One of the factors that affects the way light-sensitive cells respond is how bright the light is. A very bright light causes nerves to fire sooner than a dim light.

In this trick, both eyes are looking at a moving object. One eye is looking at it through a dark lens and the other eye is uncovered. The light coming through the lens is less bright than the light reaching the uncovered eye. The nerves in the retina of the uncovered eye fire a fraction of a second sooner than those in the eye looking through the lens. It's believed that this tiny difference in the firing of nerves in your two eyes produces the illusion of depth. The pendulum you are looking at is simply swinging from side to side. With this illusion (called the Panfrisch illusion) you see the pendulum swinging in a circular path. Sometimes it appears closer to you and sometimes farther away. This is another phenomenon that is not yet well understood.

THE SETUP

a string about three feet long
a heavy object to act as a pendulum bob
dark glasses (We used an inexpensive package of ten sunglasses that were birthday party favors. We cut the glasses in half so there were enough lenses for twenty people.)

Tie the string to the heavy object. Hang the pendulum in front of a blank wall. It should swing slowly from side to side.

THE ACT

Hand out dark lenses to members of your audience. Have them watch the pendulum swing with both eyes

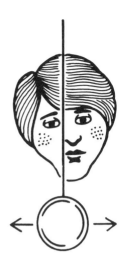

open. Ask someone to describe the path of the pendulum. Then have everyone put a dark lens in front of their right eye, keeping both eyes open. Have someone describe the motion of the pendulum. It will appear to be swinging in an oval path in a clockwise direction.

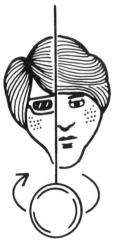

Then have everyone switch the lens to the left eye. The pendulum will appear to change its direction of rotation. It will appear to be swinging in an oval path in a counterclockwise direction.

Performance tips: This effect is great entertainment for a party.

Bizarre Boomerangs: A Size Illusion

You display two cardboard boomerangs and prove they are the same size by putting one on top of the other. Then you stretch one with your hands and, suddenly, it grows. Squeeze and it shrinks.

WHAT'S HAPPENING

An object can appear to be different sizes depending on its surroundings. One of the most famous natural illusions is the apparent change in size of a full moon as it rises. When the moon is near the horizon, it appears larger than it does later when it is overhead. If you look at the moon through a tube when it is near the horizon, it appears no larger than when it is overhead. Scientists think the reason the moon looks larger when it is near the horizon is because it is near objects we're used to seeing.

In this trick, the illusion that one boomerang is larger than the other is created by holding the smaller arc of one boomerang above the larger arc of the other. The two arcs which are next to each other are different in size, so the two boomerangs look different in size. The lower boomerang appears to be larger. This illusion is so reliable that even proof that the boomerangs are exactly the same size cannot change your perception that the upper boomerang is smaller than the lower one.

THE SETUP

    7-inch paper plates
    a pin
    a pencil
    scissors

Find the center of a paper plate as you did for Benham's Top (pg. 144). Draw a pie-shaped wedge that extends to the center and includes about one-third of the plate. Cut this piece out.

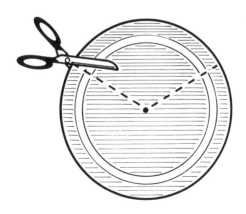

Use the outside arc of another plate as a pattern and draw an arc on the pie-shaped piece so that the straight edges are about one and one-half inches long. Cut the plate along the smaller arc to form the boomerang. Use this boomerang as a pattern to make another one.

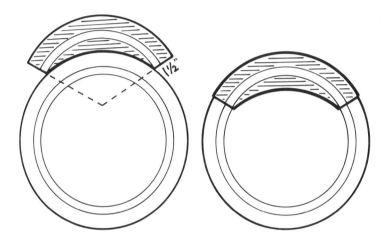

THE ACT

Show your audience that the two boomerangs are exactly the same size by putting one over the other. Put one boomerang down on the table. Pretend to stretch the other one. Show how the stretching has worked by comparing it to the boomerang you've left on the table. When you compare boomerangs, be sure to put the boomerang you pretended to stretch *under* the other boomerang.

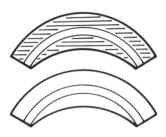

Performance tips: You can elaborate on the trick by pretending to shrink the boomerang. When you put it back down, put it *above* the other boomerang, so it appears smaller than the one you haven't touched.

Index

Entries in italics are names of tricks.

156

About the Author

Vicki Cobb attended the University of Wisconsin on a Ford Foundation Early Admissions Scholarship, then continued her education at Barnard College, where she received her B.A. degree, and at Columbia University Teachers College, where she was awarded an M.A. degree.

After an early career as a science teacher, Ms. Cobb turned to writing film strips and other educational aids. She was the creator and principal personality of "The Science Game," an educational television series, and is presently a television script writer. Her books for young people include *Science Experiments You Can Eat*, *Arts and Crafts You Can Eat*, *Supersuits*, and *How the Doctor Knows You're Fine*.

About the Illustrator

Lance R. Miyamoto, a graduate of Philadelphia College of Art, is a young free-lance illustrator with six books to his credit. His artwork has also appeared in such national credit. His artwork has also appeared in *Cue*, *Signature*, *Family Health*, *Car and Driver*, and other magazines.